THE LITTLE BOOK OF
ANGELS

SOPHIE GOLDING

summersdale

THE LITTLE BOOK OF ANGELS

Text by Susan McCann

An Hachette UK Company
www.hachette.co.uk

Summersdale Publishers Ltd
Part of Octopus Publishing Group Limited
Carmelite House
50 Victoria Embankment
LONDON
EC4Y 0DZ
UK

www.summersdale.com

Printed and bound in the UK

ISBN: 978-1-80007-694-5

Substantial discounts on bulk quantities of Summersdale books are available to corporations, professional associations and other organizations. For details contact general enquiries: telephone: +44 (0) 1243 771107 or email: enquiries@summersdale.com.

CONTENTS

INTRODUCTION

People have always sought some sort of spiritual guidance, and though many of us will have a preconceived idea of what angels are, this book explores all types of spirit guides from different religions and cultures, as well as the gifts they can bring to your life here on earth.

We'll explore the meaning and history of angels across many ancient and mainstream religions, along with other types of spirit guides more akin to modern spirituality, giving tips on how to recognize them. This book will also help you to discover how to connect with angels and understand how they can provide comfort, protection, guidance, healing and much more in both everyday life and in times of crisis.

In many world religions, Angels are often viewed as spiritual beings who connect us with our specific god or deities, an intermediary between earth and heaven or the spiritual realm. Angels appear in many religious legends, fro m Archangel Gabriel's visit to the Virgin Mary, in Christianity, to Angel Jibril dictating the Qur'an to Mohammad, in Islam. It is comforting to know that whatever religious or spiritual belief we hold, we too can access our own guardian angels or spirit guides whenever we choose.

ANGELS MEND
OUR PATCHWORK
HEARTS WITH
THREADS OF LOVE.

TERRI GUILLEMETS

A HISTORY OF ANGELS

Angelology – the study of angels – is a fascinating and thriving area that continues to have enormous relevance in our modern world. While it may not be possible to pinpoint an exact time in history when the concept of angels or celestial beings began, these messengers, believed to be sent by a god or deity, have formed part of the belief systems of cultures all over the world since ancient times. This chapter gives a brief overview of how angels have been perceived throughout history. It looks at angel systems and hierarchies in religions including Christianity, Judaism, Islam and Zoroastrianism (a pre-Islamic religion of ancient Persia) and explores celestial beings in Buddhism and Hinduism, as well as the concept of divine messengers in ancient thought.

WHAT ARE ANGELS?

Belief in angels spans multiple religions, but in all of them an angel is a spiritual being who worships and serves their god or deity. They are often seen as being an intermediary between their god and humanity, delivering divine messages and protecting and guiding their human charges.

What religions believe in angels?

Ancient Western religions, such as Zoroastrianism, Judaism, Christianity and Islam, view the cosmos as a tripartite universe (composed of earth, heaven and hell) and have a longstanding belief in angels. These religions are all monotheistic, meaning they believe in the existence of only one god. Other cultures, such as Buddhism and Hinduism, may not explicitly reference angels but have a belief in similar celestial beings, divine messengers or deities.

The word "angel" comes from the Greek *angelos*, meaning "messenger".

ANGELIC RANKS IN CHRISTIANITY

The most commonly used system of organizing angels worldwide is the Pseudo-Dionysius angelic hierarchy, which ranks angels from highest to lowest:

1. Seraphim
2. Cherubim
3. Thrones
4. Dominions (or dominations)
5. Virtues
6. Powers
7. Principalities
8. Archangels
9. Angels

Grouping by sphere

- **The first circle** – the seraphim, cherubim and thrones are closest to God and spend their time contemplating him.

- **The second circle** – the dominions, virtues and powers are said to govern the universe.

- **The third circle** – principalities, archangels and angels are believed to carry out the orders of the higher-ranked angels and be the medium between God and humans.

INDIVIDUAL ANGEL RANKS IN CHRISTIANITY

- **Seraphim** – the "burning ones" guard God's throne in heaven and spend their time praising him, their brilliant light showing their love. Lucifer (the "light bearer") was said to have once been closest to God but fell when he coveted God's power for himself. He became a demon and is also known as Satan.

- **Cherubim** – known for their wisdom, Cherubims protect God's glory and record what happens in the universe.

- **Thrones** – concerned with carrying out God's justice, Thrones look to correct wrongs on earth.

- **Dominions** – these supervise the other angels in carrying out their duties. Dominions also channel God's love to others in the universe.

- **Virtues** – these angels watch over the natural world and help humans strengthen their belief in God. They are the ones who carry out miracles on earth both at God's command and in response to prayers.

- **Powers** – these carry out spiritual warfare against demons, helping earthlings overcome temptation and motivating them with the courage to choose good over evil.

- **Principalities** – these angels encourage prayer and spiritual discipline and provide inspiration in the arts and sciences. Principalities oversee the nations on earth and try to carry wisdom to national leaders.

- **Archangels** – contrary to popular belief, archangels are actually placed in the second-lowest rank according to theological works, due to their proximity to humankind. This choir is comprised of angels who deliver messages from God to us earthlings, including some of the archangels that we are more familiar with (such as Michael and Gabriel). Christians now consider Michael to be the most powerful angel.

- **Angels** – these are the closest angelic beings to humans. Guardian angels belong to this choir, protecting and guiding us.

WHAT ARE DIVINE MESSENGERS?

Sometimes we receive what we might describe as "divine messages": an intuition, feeling, image or message appearing in our mind from nowhere. We might receive these through omens or dreams, or through messengers who stand between humans and the divine, such as angels or other spirit guides.

What are deities?

The Oxford English Dictionary describes a deity as a "god or goddess", meaning that they have divine status. Deities can be found in polytheistic religions that worship multiple gods and goddesses, such as Hinduism or Paganism. Whatever we may call them, angels, divine messengers or deities are there to assist, comfort and help us feel closer to God or the divine.

> The word "angel" has similar roots across the globe. The "-el" originates from the Hebrew word for God and signifies that the name bearer comes from God. Fallen angels are not privy to this special suffix.

MAKE YOUR WISH
AND LET YOUR
ANGELS CARRY YOUR
DREAMS ON THEIR
LOVING WINGS

DEITIES IN ANCIENT EGYPT

Dating back to around 3,150 BCE, the Egyptian deities Horus (the Falcon God) and Isis are both winged, which was thought to signify angelic abilities. Ancient Egyptians believed that Horus' vast wings symbolized the heavens, and Horus himself was said to have appeared as a winged sun disc to attack and kill the sun god Ra's enemies. Wings became crucial in Egyptian thinking and ideology, and the open wings of deities symbolized their ability to enclose and protect. The striking image of the winged sun disc is still popular today and symbolizes protection against chaos.

The Babylonians and Hittites later also adopted this powerful image. The sun disc is thought to resemble the thrones in Christian angelology, or "wheels of fire". These creatures are portrayed as the wheels of God's chariot and contain many eyes. They are said to maintain cosmic harmony, administering divine justice and keeping universal laws in balance.

DIVINE MESSENGERS IN ANCIENT GREECE

Around 2,500 years ago, Ancient Greeks had a strong belief in divine messengers who sometimes reached them with enigmatic and otherworldly messages through their dreams. The word "daemon" (from the Ancient Greek verb *daiesthai*, meaning to divide or distribute) was used by the Greek philosopher Plato to describe divine messengers in a positive light. In Plato's book *Apology*, Socrates described what we would know today as a guardian angel. He believed that humans could have a personal daemon, who would be with them for life and could determine a person's fate. Socrates described how he was frequently warned by his own daemon's "voice" when he was about to make a mistake or encounter danger, though his daemon never told him how to act, only advising him.

The Greek god Hermes (known to the Romans as Mercury) sported wings and was known as the messenger of the gods.

DIVINE MESSENGERS IN OTHER ANCIENT CULTURES

Sumeria and Babylonia

One of the earliest divine messengers was Anzû, who appeared in early Mesopotamian religious culture and resembled a cat-headed eagle-vulture. Anzû means "to have knowledge of the divine", and was the connection between the divine and mortal realms. Altars dedicated to winged guardian angels have been found by archaeologists in ancient Sumeria (modern-day Iraq) and dated to 3000 BCE.

Ancient Persia

In all ancient cultures, storytelling was the most prevalent way of recording history. Many of the deities revered in ancient Persia later appeared in the works of Zoroastrianism, the oldest monotheistic religion, which came into prominence around 1500–1000 BCE. Ancient Persian lore described divine messengers, such as Neriosang, an angel and messenger of the gods, and Nairyosangha, an angel associated with fire and purity who carries prayers from earth to heaven and was said to be the supreme being Ahura Mazda's messenger (see pages 18–19 on Zoroastrianism).

EVEN WHEN
MUDDY YOUR
WINGS SPARKLE
BRIGHT WONDERS
THAT HEAL
BROKEN WORLDS.

ABERJHANI

ANGELS IN ZOROASTRIANISM

The ancient faith of Zoroastrianism predates Christianity and was founded by the Persian prophet Zarathustra (whose Greek name was Zoroaster) around 600 BCE. Ahura Mazda (Wise Lord) is the supreme being, and the faith also recognizes archangels (*amesha spentas*), angels (*yazata*) and guardian angels (*fravashis*).

Amesha spentas

In Zoroastrianism, which survives today in Iran and in the minority Indian Parsi community, *amesha spentas* (or beneficent immortals) are seven archangels – the highest spiritual beings created by Ahura Mazda – through which all subsequent creation was achieved.

Yazata

An order of *yazata* is believed to have been created by Ahura Mazda to help him maintain world order and destroy the evil spirit Ahriman and his demons. *Yazata* are said to gather the light of the sun and pour it on the earth, assisting humans to purify themselves and grow. Most of the main *yazata* are former ancient Iranian deities, now allocated a more minor status: Anahita (the ancient Persian goddess of fertility, water, wisdom, healing), Ātar (symbolizing fire), Mithra (truth), Rashnu (justice and the righteous), Sraosha (Ahura Mazda's divine messenger) and Verethraghna (the spirit of victory). Zoroastrians, of whom there are an estimated 110,000 worldwide today, choose an angel to protect them and dedicate their prayers to that angel throughout their lives. Making ritual offerings to their angel, they believe, helps them receive its favour and brings prosperity.

Fravashis

In Zoroastrianism, each person is accompanied by a *fravashi* to guide them throughout life. They were said to have guarded the boundaries of heaven but now volunteer to accompany souls to earth to protect them. Zoroastrians can invoke their guardian angel for help whenever they find themselves in danger or need of guidance. The soul is expected to strive for the *fravashi* ideal, merging with it after death. *Fravashis* are said to manifest God's energy, preserve order and fly like winged birds. They are symbolized as a winged disk (influenced by the ancient Egyptian symbol), often with a person superimposed. This is known as the Faravahar.

ANGELS IN JUDAISM

Around 540 BCE, the Hebrew people left Babylon and brought their belief in angels with them. Like Zoroastrianism, Judaism divides the universe into earth, heaven and hell. Angels in both religions link heaven with earth, carrying out God's will, rewarding the good and punishing sin and injustice. They help humans understand God's will and take the souls of the virtuous to heaven.

Inspired by Zoroastrianism, the Old Testament god Yahweh has an army of angels who battle evil forces led by Satan (known as Ahriman in Zoroastrianism). Jewish scriptures only name Michael, Gabriel and Raphael, but later Judaism refers to other angel types, such as the Angel of Death, and proclaims there to be seven archangels that lead unnamed, heavenly messengers. Later tradition gives us Raguel, Remiel or Jeremiel, Sariel and Uriel.

By the fourth century, more angels had been named in mainstream Judaism and in the Kabbalah, a mystical branch of Judaism. Some had special traits, such as Kafziel (the right to conquer), and nations had their own angels, such as Persia's Dubbiel or "Bear of God". However, they were all tasked with doing God's work and had no free will.

In the fifth and sixth centuries CE, the inhabitants of Babylonia used incantation bowls to pray to angels. In her book, *On My Right Michael, On My Left Gabriel: Angels in Ancient Jewish Culture*, Professor Mika Ahuvia found that 40 per cent of the bowls she studied contained pleas to the angels for help with problems such as gossip, curses, physical illness and marital issues, alongside requests to God. The most popular prayer was one against meddling in-laws, an issue that God may have considered trivial but that was no less irritating for his people. Angels would have been useful for these daily annoyances – perhaps not much has changed today!

THE JEWISH ANGELS HIERARCHY

Around 1180 CE, Jewish philosopher Maimonides (also known as Moshe ben Maimon), a Rabbi and scholar of the Torah, described the Jewish hierarchy of angels in his book *Mishneh Torah*. There are ten levels of angels, ranked from highest to lowest:

1. **Chayot ha kodesh** – radiating a powerful and fiery light, the highest and most enlightened angels hold earth in its position in space, as well as holding up God's throne. According to the Kabbalah, they are led by Archangel Metatron.

2. **Ophanim** – these wise angels guard God's throne in heaven 24/7 and are said to never sleep. Their name originates from the Hebrew *ophan* (wheel). In the Torah (Ezekiel Chapter 1), their spirits are described as being encased inside wheels. In the Kabbalah, they are led by Archangel Raziel.

3. **Erelim** – courageous and understanding, in the Kabbalah the *erelim* are led by Archangel Tzaphkiel and can be called upon in times of national tragedy or at the moment of death.

4. **Hashmallim** – led by Archangel Zadkiel, the *hashmallim* promote love, kindness and grace.

5. **Seraphim** – led by Archangel Chamuel, *seraphims* work to achieve justice.

6. **Malakhim** – led by Archangel Raphael, *malakhim* are messengers, delivering God's word to the human race, and are said to be both beautiful and merciful.

7. **Elohim** – led by Archangel Haniel, the *elohim* are committed to assuring the victory of good over evil.

8. **Bene elohim** – the *bene elohim* give glory to God and are led by Archangel Michael. Michael is the angel most mentioned across major religious texts and is often portrayed as a warrior who fights for what's right in order to bring glory to God. In the Torah, Michael is described as "the great prince" who will protect God's people even at the end of the world, during the struggle between good and evil (Daniel 12:21).

9. **Cherubim** – helping people process and heal their sins in order to draw closer to God, the *cherubim* are led by Archangel Gabriel.

10. **Ishim** – these angels build God's kingdom on earth and are the closest to us earthlings. Their leader is Archangel Sandalphon.

OTHER ANGELS IN JUDAISM

Archangels in Judaism

Archangels don't have a Hebrew equivalent in Jewish Scriptures, but in the Book of Daniel, Michael and Gabriel are both mentioned by name and described as "ministers", differentiating them from unnamed angels that are later encountered in the Bible, from Genesis onwards.

Guardian angels in Judaism

Appearing in later Rabbinic tradition is the idea that everyone has two angels, one watching out for the good things you do and one looking out for the sins you commit. It's said that the two "guardian angels" come before God on judgement day to argue your case.

Sikhs believe in one god and do not make explicit reference to angels or other supernatural beings. However, the Guru Granth Sahib, the scared scripture of the Sikhs, mentions Azrael (sometimes known as Yam), describing him as the messenger or angel of death. Chitar and Gupat are also mentioned, described as angels who record the conscious and unconscious thoughts and actions of all mortal beings.

ANGELS IN CHRISTIANITY

Inspired by Judaic and Zoroastrian ideas, Christians also believe in angels and a tripartite universe. Seen as God's messengers, they play a sizeable role in the daily lives of many Christians, from delivering prayers to God, to bringing strength and comfort. Innumberable angels are thought to exist – more than we could ever count.

Angel hierarchy

Around 500 CE, the Greek philosopher and theologian Pseudo-Dionysius the Areopagite published *The Celestial Hierarchy*, detailing the angelic hierarchy from studying the Bible. This was fleshed out by theologian Thomas Aquinas in his book *Summa Theologica*, published posthumously in 1485. Angels are split into different types, levels, powers and appearances. Both books ranked angels into nine choirs, each grouped into a triad. Angels are said to inhabit spheres of power that surround God, meaning three choirs are allocated to each of the three spheres. Those closest to God inhabit the inner sphere, with those closest to humans inhabiting the outer sphere.

ARCHANGELS IN CHRISTIANITY

Although theological texts place archangels amongst the lower-ranking angels, Christians often consider them to be the highest-ranking ones in heaven. In *Paradise Lost*, a seventeenth-century poem by John Milton, archangels are given the highest rank and this may have something to do with how they are viewed today in popular consciousness.

In Christianity, God is believed to give archangels the most significant responsibilities. The word "archangel" is derived from the Greek *arkhi* (ruler) and *angelos* (messenger), showing the archangels' dual role: they rule over other angels, but also deliver messages to humankind from God.

The number of archangels in existence is debated among different faiths, but it's generally accepted that there are seven major archangels who supervise a team of angels specializing in a particular area (for example, healing). These teams of angels work on one of seven particular light ray frequencies (see page 110 for more information on these frequencies and how to connect to them).

Said to be made of pure love, the seven best-known archangels are:

- **Archangel Michael** – the leader, known for his warrior instincts. In the Bible, Torah and the Qur'an, Michael leads the battle against evil. Call on him for protection in any situation. He will also direct you to the most appropriate archangel for your needs.

- **Archangel Gabriel** – the famous Messenger (or Angel of Revelation) helps you receive and understand messages from God.

- **Archangel Raphael** – known as the Healer, Raphael assists in healing all of God's creations, including humans and animals.

- **Archangel Uriel** – known as the Transformer, Uriel is full of wisdom, shining light on the truth and giving support during change.

- **Archangel Ariel** – Known as the archangel of nature, Ariel works with the natural elements, as well as healing animals and plants, and strengthening the relationship between humans and the natural world.

- **Archangel Chamuel** – the Nurturer, Chamuel teaches love of the self and of others.

- **Archangel Zadkiel** – known as the Forgiver, Zadkiel can help with compassion and forgiveness.

ARCHANGELS AS COMPASS POINTS AND NATURAL ELEMENTS

Many believers consider Michael, Gabriel, Raphael and Uriel to be the most important archangels. They are said to represent the four compass points and four natural elements that keep us in balance.

Uriel: north and earth

Uriel can bring stability to your earthly life and balance to relationships, assisting with practical solutions to problems and helping you to ground and utilize spiritual knowledge and wisdom.

Michael: south and fire

Michael's key work is in the areas of truth and courage. Fire provides illumination and can guide us towards the revelation of spiritual truth, while the "blazing fire" of passion for serving God and living your authentic truth can give us the courage to overcome our fears. Fire is said to assist humans to burn away their sins, and as fire is associated with the concept of hell, this reminds believers that Michael is a warrior who fights evil.

Raphael: east and air

Raphael empowers you to soar towards your life purpose and goals, helping you to break free from unhealthy habits and situations to become who you are truly meant to be. He inspires you to lift your soul towards God.

Gabriel: west and water

One of Gabriel's missions is to communicate God's messages and help us receive them with clarity, just as water is clear. We also use water for purification; Gabriel assists us to reflect on our thoughts and emotions, and to pursue a pure life in order to become closer to God.

Each archangel's name is related to its duty. Most of the names end with the suffix "-el" ("in God"). The rest of the name signifies the specialism of that archangel. For example, the meaning of Uriel is "God is my light", and Uriel shines the light of divine spiritual knowledge and wisdom in the darkness. Raphael's name means "God heals", appropriate to his divine duties.

ARCHANGELS IN TAROT CARDS

Yes, our four omnipresent archangels appear in tarot readings, too! Tarot cards have been an established divining tool since the fifteenth century and many people still turn to a card reading for advice about present situations and what could potentially happen in the future.

Archangel Michael – Temperance
Michael is said to be found on the Temperance card, which shows balance and harmony as well as the connection of the spiritual and physical realms.

Archangel Gabriel – Judgement
As befits Gabriel's duties as the Angel of Revelation, the angel blowing a trumpet on the Judgement card is said to be him. Here he represents spiritual communication, awakenings and resurrections.

Raphael – The Lovers
As part of his healing duties, Raphael is said to watch over those looking for soulmates – whether romantic or platonic, he is said to be able to help you make the perfect connection, healing your heart.

Uriel – The Devil

The meaning of Uriel's name ("God is my light") and the fact that he shines light on wisdom, knowledge and spiritual truth, shows us – through this card representing darkness – that we can be freed from suffering. This card can shed light on the illusions that keep us trapped, helping us grow in wisdom and learn from our mistakes.

What do angels look like?

Most religions accept that angels may appear either in human or heavenly form. For example, a stranger who appeared from nowhere to help you in your hour of need could have been an angel in human form. Other angels are thought to appear as they're often depicted in art, as our brains are more likely to perceive something in a form we're familiar with. In Judaism, an angel is a spiritual being with no physical attributes. The wings and arms seen by the prophets are metaphorical and refer to their abilities and tasks.

ARCHANGELS IN WORLD RELIGIONS

Zoroastrianism, Judaism, Christianity and Islam all acknowledge powerful archangels in their religious doctrines and traditions, although they disagree on the finer details. Some texts mention more of them than others.

Archangels are usually referred to or thought of as male, but this could be an antiquated way of viewing them when concepts were often recorded in the male gender by default. Some believers in current times see Archangel Jophiel, for example, the archangel of beauty and wisdom, as a female presence or energy, while others believe angels, as inhabitants of the spiritual realm, to be beyond gender. They are said to be able to appear to humans in any form of their choosing, perhaps according to what the believer desires or will recognize, or the form that will help them accomplish their mission most successfully.

KABBALAH AND THE TREE OF LIFE

Followers of Kabbalah work with ten branches of the Tree of Life. Each "sephirot" (branch) has a divine name:

Kether, meaning "the crown" –
Archangel Metatron directs God's energy

Chokmah, meaning "wisdom" –
Archangel Raziel reveals divine wisdom

Binah, meaning "understanding" –
Archangel Tzaphkiel sends compassion

Chesed, meaning "mercy" –
Archangel Zadkiel supervises God's mercy

Geburah, meaning "strength" –
Archangel Chamuel strengthens relationships

Tiphareth or Tifereth, meaning "beauty" –
Archangel Raphael expresses the divine energy of beauty

Netzach, meaning "eternity" –
Archangel Haniel brings joy and enlightenment

Hod, meaning "glory" –
Archangel Michael expresses God's glory

Yesod, meaning "the foundation" –
Archangel Gabriel promotes communication

Malkuth or Malkhuth, meaning "the kindom" –
Archangel Sandalphon encourages music and prayer

ANGELS IN ISLAM

Islam recognizes a hierarchy of angels, similar in idea to Judaic and Christian beliefs. Although it is less detailed, archangels are the highest-ranking angels, with other angels placed below them, differentiated by mission. Many Muslims believe that *malaikah*, or angels, were conceived before humans, then tasked with communicating with them and following Allah's orders.

These angels are immortal beings with wings, who are made of light. They are so pure that they do not sin and are able to appear in human form. However, where Judaism and Christianity categorize angels into those who are with God and those who have fallen, Islam recognizes angels, demons and *djinni* (genies). *Djinni* were created from fire and can be either harmful or good, visible or invisible. They are also said to be capable of assuming human or animal forms.

Angels:

- escort good Muslims into paradise and oversee the pits of hell.

- act as messengers to the prophets.

- guide and protect people.

- record everything a human does, for use on the Day of Judgement.

ALLOW YOUR
ANGELS TO
TRANSFORM
YOUR WORRIES

PROMINENT MUSLIM ANGELS

- **Izrail**, also known as the Angel of Death, delivers human souls to the afterlife.

- **Jibril** (Gabriel), the bearer of good news, considered the most important of the archangels. He is said to have dictated the Qur'an to the prophet Muhammad.

- **Mika'il** (Michael) provides food and rain, rewarding those who do good deeds. Also known as the Angel of Mercy, he asks Allah to forgive people's sins.

- **Israfil** (Raphael) will announce Judgement Day and be present on the day of resurrection.

- **Munkar** and **Nakir** are said to question a mortal's soul after death.

Guardian angels in Islam

The Muslim faith believes that everyone has two guardian angels, known as the Kiraman Katibin (honourable recorders). They accompany their charges for life and observe everything that they do, say and think once they have reached adolescence. The angel on the right records the person's good choices and deeds, while the angel on the left records the bad actions and decisions. Muslims sometimes look at both shoulders during prayer, saying "Peace be upon you" in acknowledgement of their guardian angels.

BUDDHIST DEITIES

In Buddhist philosophy, devas are celestial beings who rank above humans but differ from the angels of Western religions. The word deva means "shining ones" in Sanskrit, and it's believed that every person, animal and plant has a deva (male) or devi (female), a form of divine energy, to protect and nurture it. Mahayana Buddhists, meanwhile, believe in transcendent bodhisattvas, angelic beings who protect humans and amplify their prayers.

Buddhist devas:

- are not immortal

- are distinct individuals with their own personalities and life paths, though higher-order devas radiate their own light and float, while some have no physical form, existing only in meditation

- act in similar ways to guardian angels but their knowledge is inferior to that of a fully enlightened Buddha

- are not morally perfect

- have no role in shaping the world and are subject to the same universal laws of cause and effect as any other being

IT IS IMPOSSIBLE TO SEE THE ANGEL UNLESS YOU FIRST HAVE A NOTION OF IT.

JAMES HILLMAN

DEVAS IN HINDUISM

Like Buddhism, Hinduism also recognizes celestial beings. There are major gods, such as Lord Krishna, who is the god of protection, compassion, tenderness and love, minor gods (devas or devis), human gurus (those who have become enlightened spiritual teachers) and deceased ancestors. Brahma, Vishnu and Shiva are said to form the Hindu trinity, the Trimurthi. They oversee the evolution and function of the universe.

There are also lesser devas in charge of the forces of nature, such as Varuna, the god of water, Vayu, the god of the wind and Agni, the god of fire. Other celestial beings include lipika (who govern karma), gandharvas (male celestial singers), apsaras (female celestial dancers and nymphs) and angiris (who oversee sacrifices).

Many devas are benevolent, but there are also evil spirits or demons, known as asuras. These fallen devas can be a harmful influence in someone's spiritual journey, but they can be reincarnated into devas if they do good deeds.

THE ANGEL OF MONS

World War I (1914–1919)

In August 1914, as British and French soldiers retreated from the Germans at Mons, Belgium, troops described seeing a tall, serene-looking blond man dressed in golden armour. French soldiers thought it was Archangel Michael, whilst the British believed it to be Saint George.

The Allied army was hopelessly outnumbered, but later reports from the Germans suggested they were unable to advance and that their horses turned and ran, preventing an Allied massacre. The angel became known as the Angel of Mons, its myth turned into legend and the hope that it gave to the countries fighting Germany spread quickly.

While some sources put the sighting down to hysteria, the troops' lack of sleep or even wartime propaganda, many soldiers are said to have spoken of the strange events at Mons to the nurses treating their wounds.

WHEN YOU
INVITE ANGELS
INTO YOUR LIFE,
EVERYTHING
BECOMES A
LITTLE BRIGHTER

ANGELS IN MODERN TIMES

Angels are hugely popular today in many cultures all over the world, appearing in everything from popular music to lead roles on the silver screen. Statues of angels are common in gardens, fashionable on clothing and popular as jewellery charms. The modern concept of angels is not restricted to specific religions but also benefits from acceptance in the secular world. According to a survey by Baylor University in Texas, 55 per cent of Americans believe that an angel has stepped in to protect them from harm.

Today, angels are inspiring thoughtful concepts, such as National Be an Angel Day in the US, which takes place on 22 August every year. Created in 1993 by Jayne Howard Feldman, it asks us to show kindness to another or carry out a good deed, allowing angels to work through us here on earth. The day also gives us an opportunity to acknowledge and appreciate those who've been like angels to us.

ANGELS IN ART

Angels have a long history in the world of art, showing people's changing perceptions of them over time. In the Middle Ages, they were depicted in human form with bird-like wings, whereas modern art is more fluid in its interpretation, exploring angels as ethereal beings of light in varying forms and colours.

The Annunciation by Fra Angelico (1440–1445) and *The Dream of Joachim* by Giotto (1305) are famous Renaissance frescoes of angels, while *The Angel Standing in the Sun* by J.M.W. Turner (1846) and *When the Morning Stars Sang Together* by William Blake (1825) are stunning examples of angels in fine art.

Famous sculptures range from the marble-carved *Angel* by Michelangelo (1495) to *The Angel of the North*, a steel sculpture near Newcastle, UK, by Anthony Gormley (1998).

In literature, Shakespeare, Marlowe, Dante and John Milton have famously featured angels in their work, while movies such as *It's a Wonderful Life* and *City of Angels* have depicted them on screen in human form.

CHAPTER
TWO

OTHER SPIRIT GUIDES

Our traditional idea of what angels mean, and what form they may take, is expanding in today's cosmopolitan world. Angels can be found in many diverse cultural and spiritual contexts, and their innate religious ideology can often cross over with spiritual beliefs. This chapter looks at other forms that angels might take, exploring spirit guides such as guardian angels, spirit animals, ancestors, ascended masters, goddesses and starseeds, describing their characteristics and their usefulness to us mortals here on earth. We will also explore how these guides can connect with you and why they might visit.

SPIRIT GUIDES

What is a spirit guide?

A "spirit guide" is a general term often used in Western spiritualism and refers to spirit or celestial beings that can derive from non-human or human origins. They occupy the spiritual realm and are fonts of ancient wisdom that we can tap into at any time, should we wish. Spirit guides can originate from many sources, ranging from extra-terrestrial systems to guardian-angel orders, and you may not even be aware that you're working with these beings – or with which one. Your guides may or may not have spent time on earth before.

Spirit guides can take many forms, depending on what energies you feel most connected to (such as religious, interdimensional or intergalactic). These can include (but are not limited to):

- Guardian angels
- Ascended masters
- Saints
- Elementals (nature spirits)
- Starseeds
- Ancestors
- Goddesses
- Spirit animals

WHAT DOES A SPIRIT GUIDE DO?

Spirit guides perform three key tasks:

- Impart wisdom, practical and spiritual information
- Offer healing and enhance our own healing abilities
- Provide guidance and protect us from harm

We all have at least one primary spirit guide (some may call this their guardian angel) to guide and protect us for life. Other spirit guides will come and go during your lifetime as and when you need them.

A spirit guide can communicate in a number of ways. They may appear in your dreams or put ideas or messages directly into your mind; alternatively, a gut instinct or feeling calm during a moment of turmoil could be their work. If the energy or communication feels familiar, this could be a deceased relative. You might detect a spirit guide with you at times when you're sad, lonely or upset. They may also send you signs via other media like books, TV, music, other humans and angel numbers (see pages 93–99).

ARCHETYPAL GUIDES

These are guides who often appear in symbolic, traditional roles that you might recognize (for example, a shaman). They appear for a purpose, typically to teach you a lesson or guide you along a path. You may receive information during dreams or meditation. They could be with you for life or just to support you at a specific time. Some examples include:

- **A relationship guide**: if a relationship ends, that guide is no longer needed. A new guide may appear with a new relationship.

- **A trauma guide**: may be working behind the scenes to help those involved in a particular traumatic experience. Once healing is complete, the guide may leave.

We might work with a guide once or many times. Some will be experts in a particular area and come and go as needed. If the person's soul develops, they may outgrow their original mentor and begin work with a new one. So perhaps you've had a number of guides working behind the scenes in your life already.

HOW CAN I CONTACT
MY SPIRIT GUIDE?

If you'd like to connect with your guides or are looking for help in a particular area, try the following:

- Just before you go to sleep, ask your guide(s) to appear in your dream and note down any recollections or visions when you wake. Don't reject anything.

- Try a spirit-guide meditation. There are many free guided meditations online or, if you prefer to do your own, see box opposite.

- You can always ask your guide for a physical sign. It might appear anywhere and unexpectedly (such as on a TV advert, in a magazine or book, or in conversation), so stay alert.

- Some guides like to work through other tools such as runes or angel cards, so try these methods too.

- Have you ever felt something deep in your gut? If so, your guide might be trying to protect you from a bad or dangerous situation (see page 115) – trust your intuition.

- You can ask your guide explicitly for help. Keep it informal – treat your guide as a good friend to have a chat with in quiet or reflective moments.

Multiple spirit guides can advise and assist you, so know that the right guide will show itself at the right time for you.

Spirit guide meditation

1. Make yourself comfortable in a quiet place where you won't be disturbed.

2. Play some soothing music and, once your mind is stilled, ask your guide to step forward. You may see or intuit your guide with your third eye, or you may sense their presence. The third eye is located in the middle of your forehead and is the sixth of seven chakras or "energy centres" in the Indian chakra system. It's believed to provide perception beyond ordinary sight and can deepen spiritual connection.

3. Feel free to ask your guide's name. You can ask them for help with anything that's on your mind. Listen objectively to any advice they give and always remember to thank them afterwards.

HOW DO I KNOW IF I'VE CONNECTED TO A SPIRIT GUIDE?

Every now and then, you may get a negative spirit, voice or energy that's decided to drop in. This can sometimes be a part of yourself that's fearful or self-critical, but occasionally it can be something else, known as a negative entity. There's nothing to be afraid of – see page 52 for simple tips on how to get rid of any energies that you don't want to work with.

How can you tell when an entity is negative? You'll need to use your intuition, but here are some red flags to look out for:

1. If there's something that feels unpleasant, negative or "off", either energetically or in anything they say, disconnect from their guidance and say goodbye. True guides will never get angry at you or say anything spiteful.

2. The spirit is always appealing to your ego, telling you you're "special" and you're the only one exceptional enough to be privy to its wisdom.

3. It shares information of no real use, or information that makes no sense or that contravenes basic human kindness.

4. It doesn't like it if you question why it's here and what it's up to and may try to convince you that others are plotting against you, such as friends and family.

5. It may talk to you about secret portals to other worlds or claim to be from somewhere you can find no trace of.

6. It may want you to help it to do something in return for sharing "wisdom" with you.

To check if a spirit is positive or negative, ask it three times if it comes from God, Allah, Divine Source or any other supreme being or source that you regard as the truth. Any entity is bound by spiritual law to declare the truth if asked. If it says "no" on any of these occasions, it has not come from a true source and you may ask it to leave.

HOW DO I GET RID OF AN UNWANTED ENTITY?

If you are being bothered by a persistent negative entity, try the following to send it packing:

- Protect the space you're working in – cleanse it by smudging the room with sage or palo santo* or by asking Archangel Michael to protect you.

- Visualize placing protection over yourself with your third eye. This could be anything from metaphorically placing Archangel Michael's blue cloak over yourself and seeing his sword out in front of you, to placing yourself within an impenetrable golden bubble.

- Simply tell the entity to leave. It's OK to be assertive and direct. Ask it to leave and return to the light, and let it know it cannot be here.

- Cleanse and purify the space again by smudging or clapping your hands loudly in each corner of the room to send unwanted energies on their way.

*See page 107 for how to cleanse a room by smudging.

TAKE CARE OF
YOUR INNER,
SPIRITUAL
BEAUTY. THAT
WILL REFLECT
IN YOUR FACE

DOLORES DEL RÍO

SPIRIT ANIMALS

What are spirit animals?
Also known as power animals or, in Native American or shamanic tradition, animal totems, it's believed that each person has access to spirit animals that can guide, teach and protect. These are deeply connected with Mother Nature and can be high-vibrational entities that appear to share information essential to your growth. For example, a high-vibrational entity that appears in the guise of a barn owl may be guiding us toward wisdom and knowledge. Animal guides may stay with you to assist you through a major life change.

How do I find out what my spirit animal is?
Your animal guides choose you. Take note of any animals that show up in dreams or during meditation; other channels might include your intuition and telepathy, although you may also see that animal in the flesh. They may not be the animals you expect – don't be surprised if you have a snail as one of your guides instead of a lion!

HOW DO I GET TO KNOW MY SPIRIT ANIMAL?

Remember that animals have different symbolism in different cultures, so think about what this animal means to you. Get to know the animal species' qualities and behaviours; are there traits you admire, that you think would be good for you to adopt, or habits you should get rid of? What can you learn from it and the way it lives its life? Are some of those traits and behaviours relevant to things going on in your own life? Increasing familiarity with the animal will increase receptivity to its messages.

Shadow animals

A shadow-animal guide may show up in your life if you're repeating mistakes and continuing negative behaviours. It is likely to be an animal that you fear, such as a snake or wolf, and they may be showing parts of you that you're repressing or not dealing with. Once you learn to change fearful or negative behaviours, the shadow animal will disappear.

GUARDIAN ANGELS

Have you ever had a close call that should have ended in disaster but miraculously didn't? Did you feel certain that someone must have been watching out for you? Perhaps your guardian angel showed up just when you needed them.

What are guardian angels?
The Ancient Greeks and Zoroastrians believed that God assigns us all guardian angels who watch over us; similar beliefs exist in Judaism, Christianity and Islam. Guardian angels are unconditionally loving spirit guides who can point us in the right direction when needed. They are thought to protect from harm, intercede on your behalf, ask your god to help you, guide you on your path in life, and, according to some believers, record thoughts, words and deeds, handing over the information at the time of death for the universe's official records.

The ancient Mesopotamians called on the *shedu* and *lamassu* guardian spirits to protect them from evil.

HOW MANY GUARDIAN ANGELS DO YOU HAVE?

Most religions believe that everyone has at least one guardian angel, although some (such as Islam) believe that you have two, while others think that the number of guardian angels you have depends on your life circumstances and the goals your soul has set for this lifetime.

Why can't you see your guardian angel?
Guardian angels aren't physically visible to most humans, so that they don't frighten or distract us as we go about our daily lives. But just because you can't see them doesn't mean they're not there and ready to leap into action.

What is my guardian angel's personality like?
Like humans, guardian angels also have their own unique personality. Once you begin to work with them, you'll start to see their personalities and may even find yourself laughing at their jokes.

THE SPIRITUAL
LIFE DOES NOT
REMOVE US FROM
THE WORLD
BUT LEADS US
DEEPER INTO IT.

HENRI J. M. NOUWEN

YOUR GUARDIAN
ANGEL WILL
NEVER LEAVE
YOUR SIDE

HOW DO I ASK MY GUARDIAN ANGEL FOR HELP?

Experts in angelology agree that if you'd like help, simply ask for it. The way in which we ask is not important: it could be a plea, a prayer, a letter or journal entry, or you could even send a message by playing a specific song. The best way to get to know your guardian angels better is to interact with them. Having a good relationship with them can help you chart a smoother passage through life. Here are some easy ways to connect:

1. Find out their names
You may wish to connect first via prayer or meditation so that you're in a quiet, private space without external distraction. When you're comfortable and calm and your mind has cleared, ask for the name of one of your guardian angels, out loud or in your mind. The name should pop into your head. If you don't receive anything, your guardian angels could be encouraging you to name them yourself. Pick names that make you smile.

2. Ask for a sign

Angels love to communicate using signs. You can ask for one at any time, and then keep your eyes peeled over the coming days. You might see a physical sign or one that comes via your third eye in the form of a prophetic dream, vision, sudden information or knowledge, a feeling, awareness of a presence, an unexpected opportunity, human connection or a revelation about something.

3. Ask questions

Ask your angels specific questions that you need help with, for example, "How can I improve my relationship with this person?" The answer may arrive in your head immediately, or you may be given a sign a few days later. If you don't receive anything, it's important to bear in mind that your guardian angels may not know the answer, or it may be something they're not allowed to reveal to you for a higher reason you're not yet aware of.

4. Write to them

Address a letter to your guardian angels and pour out what's on your mind: perhaps you're having problems in a relationship, or there's a big decision you need to make. Your guardian angels will already know of the situation, but by writing to them you're using your free will to ask for their help. Once you've explained the problem and what you need, ask them to help in any way they're able, and then watch for guidance.

Guidance can appear in any number of forms: from intuitive insight or a gut feeling, to a voice in your head or even something that another person says to you. Always remember to thank your angels in your thoughts (or out loud), as an attitude of gratitude shows reciprocal cooperation.

As you get to know your guardian angels and the way they like to communicate with you, you'll find that recognizing their guidance will become easier.

ANCESTORS

Have you ever felt that you're being watched over by a much-loved grandparent or family member who passed away? It's allegedly common for ancestors to want to help younger members of the family make their way in life. You may not have known an ancestor-guide personally. Although they will be a blood relation, they may be from a few generations back but may wish to pass something they learned down to you.

Ancestor spirit guides connect to you through genetic memory and, depending on your beliefs, they may even fulfil the role of a guardian angel or protector for your entire lifetime. They may also be able to help in repairing generational traumas and karmic patterns, clearing the way for future generations. Our ancestors can guide, protect and heal us.

Communicating with ancestors is an ancient practice that has spanned many traditions throughout time, and they are always available to help.

HOW CAN I COMMUNICATE WITH MY ANCESTORS?

Ways to connect include daily prayer, meditation, creative pursuits such as making food, art or music, ritual ceremony and festivities, or simply by thinking of them, asking for guidance and chatting to them in your head when going about your daily activities.

Many cultures around the world honour the dead through festivities, such as the Day of the Dead (Día de los Muertos) in Latin America, while in Celtic tradition, they are honoured during the pagan festival of Samhain.

> The period from 31 October to 2 November is often considered to be the mid-point between autumn (the dying season) and winter (the death), and thus when the veil between the living and the dead is thinnest, making it an ideal time to communicate with ancestors. Known as Hallowe'en, this is a celebration in many Western cultures, though its original function, to honour and communicate with our ancestors, is now often lost.

ASCENDED MASTERS

Ascended masters reached enlightenment during their physical lifetime and transformed (ascended) to higher spiritual planes. They are tasked to help others achieve the same.

The best known are:

Jesus – teacher and healer, with a mission to bring peace

Gautama Buddha – Buddha represents wisdom

Maitreya – embodies kindness, promotes universal love and enlightenment

Melchizedek – a high priest, said to hold the secrets of God and the universe

Kuan Yin – Chinese goddess of compassion, mercy and kindness

Mahavatar Babaji – Indian yogi, guru and saint, alleged to remain in human form to assist humanity

Confucius – concerned with harmony and divine order within the family and society

Lady Nada – represents peace, service, brotherhood and divine love

St Germain – associated with transformation, alchemy and the violet flame (see next page)

VIOLET FLAME MEDITATION

The powerful violet-flame energy is said to be able to cut through all the negative dross we've accumulated in our energy field and release it, allowing us to occupy a higher-vibrational energy state. This allows us to live our daily lives in a clearer, more positive way and draws more good energies towards us, lightening both our emotional load and our mood. The meditation is quick to do and can be used for healing as it is said to release lower-vibration energies such as anger, pain, frustration or resentment. Healing is understood to occur at a cellular and spiritual level.

1. Prepare for meditation in your usual way. Settle into a comfortable position where you won't be disturbed. Light incense or a candle, focus on your breathing or play soothing music to still your mind. Once you feel calm, call on St Germain.

2. Visualize a beam of white light shining down from the heavens.

3. Imagine the white light entering the top of your head and watch as the light flows down through

your body until it connects into the earth beneath you.

4. Reverse the flow of the white light and feel it coming up through the earth, passing through your body until it connects with the heavens or the divine.

5. Now imagine a violet flame surrounding your body. Focus on the beautiful, bright violet colour and feel it burning through you (this flame carries no heat and burns as a cool flame).

6. Breathe in and see the light penetrating every cell of your body. As you breathe out, imagine that you're releasing any negativity and watch as it turns into positive, radiant energy.

7. When you're ready, allow the violet light to expand and gradually fill the room. (This may take practice.)

8. When you feel that you've finished, give thanks and gently ground yourself by imagining roots growing from your feet into the earth.

SAINTS

Saints lived human lives, during which they followed Jesus, doing good deeds and leading by example. Saints are believed to go straight to heaven after death. They often devoted their lives to God and service to others, such as the nun Mother Teresa (1910–1997), who spent her life caring for the sick and the poor. Other saints have suffered through martyrdom (St Perpetua) or were known for their humility (St Francis of Assisi) or wisdom (St Augustine).

Many believers have found comfort, inspiration and courage from the way saints lived their lives. Catholics often ask specific saints to pray for them and intercede with God on their behalf. Some of the best-known saints are patrons of particular causes or professions, for example, Catholics pray to St Peter for forgiveness, and he is also the patron saint of fishermen (as he was one in life), as well as shipbuilders, netmakers and locksmiths. He's also said to hold the keys to heaven.

WHO DECIDES WHO BECOMES A SAINT?

Before Pope John XV devised a formal process of canonization in the tenth century, it used to be the public who decided on their saints. At least two miracles – when they are said to have interceded with God on behalf of a living mortal – must be attributed to the individual after they have died. The overwhelming majority of those chosen as saints are canonized, but the Apostles are said to have received their title through acclamation – universal recognition of their holiness. There are more than 10,000 saints recognized by the Roman Catholic Church.

How can I connect with a saint?

1. Find a saint that resonates with you and study their life, words and deeds.

2. Connect with them via prayer and allow your relationship with them to grow as you develop in your own wisdom and practice.

3. Be receptive during feast days, when the contributions of each particular saint are celebrated.

AS YOU JOURNEY
THROUGH LIFE,
YOU ARE LOVED
AND PROTECTED
EVERY STEP OF
THE WAY

SAINTS AND ARCHANGELS

Saints have usually lived a human life before acquiring their heavenly status, but Archangels Michael, Gabriel and Raphael are also considered to be saints. In this capacity, they assist according to their speciality.

Saint Michael – Michael is said to be the go-to saint for those who are unwell and who work in dangerous conditions, such as police officers or prison wardens. You can also call on Michael to help you overcome a challenge and he will lead you toward victory.

Saint Gabriel – having trouble communicating or understanding someone, or perhaps even understanding your place in the world and your relationship with your god? The patron saint of communication can help you out.

Saint Raphael – this all-round healer helps with concerns regarding physical, mental, emotional and spiritual health. Connect with this patron saint to receive healing energy or advice.

GODDESSES

Goddesses are worshipped around the world in many different cultures and can be called upon in a variety of situations. Although worship of female deities, from Gaia to Diana, goes back to ancient times, a "goddess movement" emerged in the 1970s in response to male-dominated organized religions to reclaim divine feminine energy in religion and spiritual practices. Most associate working with goddesses as a neopagan practice, although followers of traditional religions are also drawn to work with specific female energies for a more rounded religious practice.

While goddesses were largely ignored from the Dark Ages onward, due to the command of the Church in Western cultures, today people of all genders are recognizing the need for both male and female divine energies to create balance in their lives. Mother Mary and Shekina, the lesser-known female Holy Spirit, are celebrated figures of Christianity.

Goddesses can be found on oracle cards and on specialist Goddess tarot cards, too.

HOW TO CONNECT WITH A GODDESS

Connecting with a goddess's divine, feminine energy can help deepen your connection with nature and lead to a more balanced life.

- Start by finding a list of goddesses and deciding which one(s) resonate with you.

- Goddesses are associated with nature and Mother Earth. Take time to respect the sacred energies of nature, and you will come closer to understanding the secrets of the goddess.

- Embody the energies of the divine feminine within your daily life. This means living a more balanced life with a focus on self-care and, sometimes, standing up to fight your corner. Warrior goddesses like Sekhmet or Kali can help with the latter.

- Dedicate an altar in your home to your favourite goddess to create a peaceful and high-vibration space. Here you can carry out any rituals that feel personal to you, for example, chanting or meditation.

WELL-KNOWN GODDESSES

Below are some goddesses you may wish to connect with:

Gaia
Worshipped by Ancient Greeks
The mother of all creation, or Mother Earth, it is believed that Gaia was born from chaos at the beginning of time into an empty universe and gave birth to the gods and the elements.

Epona
Worshipped by Romans, Celts, Gauls
As the goddess of mares and foals, the Romans are understood to have made sacrifices to Epona before battle, ensuring successful conquest. Images of Epona riding a mare also became the symbol for peaceful transition into death, but due to the status symbol of horses, she also came to symbolize prosperity.

Xochiquetzal
Worshipped by Aztecs
Xochiquetzal is often depicted surrounded by butterflies, hummingbirds and flowers and is associated with fertility, pregnancy, sex for both reproduction and pleasure, dancing and domestic creativity. She's the fun, pleasure-seeking goddess that we can thank for the invention of chocolate.

Fuji
Worshipped by Japanese

Fuji gave her name to the volcano, Mount Fuji, and is the goddess of fire. Worshippers look to placate her so that they can experience her warm, benevolent side instead of her explosive scorching one.

Other popular goddesses:

Isis – Egyptian mother goddess, also associated with nature, magic and creativity

Quan Yin – Chinese goddess of mercy and compassion

Fortuna – Roman goddess of fortune

Freya – Norse goddess of fertility, sexual liberty, abundance and war

Pelé – Hawaiian volcano goddess, both destroyer and creator

Amaterasu – Japanese goddess of the sun

Durga – Hindu Divine Mother

Sedna – Inuit goddess of the sea and queen of the underworld

Shekina – Hebrew goddess of compassion

Kali – Hindu goddess of female empowerment, time, change, death and destruction

Nut – Egyptian goddess of life, death and rebirth, said to be the sky covered in stars

Spider Grandmother – Native American goddess revered for her wisdom and leadership

SOME SPIRIT GUIDES YOU MAY NOT EVEN KNOW YOU HAVE

- **Healing guide** – this guide will show up as a healer of some kind. They could be a medical professional, a shaman or ascended master or even a massage therapist. They can provide us with healing when we most need it. They may appear spiritually or in human form, as if they're an angel on earth.

- **Warrior, soldier or other protector** – these help to protect you at all levels and filter any advice you receive to make sure you're able to differentiate the good from the bad They're most likely to communicate through gut feelings that something's not right.

- **Teacher guide** – usually here to show us a lesson, especially if we've deviated from our path. Yes, that means teachers can bring "good" and "bad" experiences, but they're here to help us learn and find the correct course to move forward.

- **Creative guide** – these are your cheerleaders when it comes to using your talents for the greater good.

- **Gatekeeper** – these guides offer protection to those

working with the spirit realm and are also said to hold the Akashic Records (everything that's occurred in the past, present and potential future).

- **Helper guide** – these guides work with many souls and will be there to help you achieve a particular goal or assist you in a certain relationship. Because they help with a specific thing, once their mission is complete they move on to help others.

- **Divine timing guide** – responsible for synchronicities, such as angel numbers (see page 93–99), and allowing your plans to unfold at the right time.

- **Joy guide** – these beautiful spirit guides encourage you to see the joy in every moment, and they love it when you laugh.

There are many more spirit guides who will show up in your life at different times to assist you with anything from changing a car tyre or sitting an exam to plucking up the courage to speak to someone for the first time.

WHAT I KNOW
FOR SURE IS THAT
WHEN SOMEONE
CLOSE TO YOU
PASSES, YOU
NOW HAVE AN
ANGEL YOU CAN
CALL BY NAME.

OPRAH WINFREY

ELEMENTAL SPIRITS

Elementals are thought to be nature spirits that inhabit rivers, trees, mountains and other spaces in nature. According to quantum physics, everything possessing mass is made of energy, and therefore everything vibrates, from humans to trees. Communication with spirit guides travels as vibrational energy, from one entity to another. This is how elemental spirits or energies communicate. They are said to take four forms:

Sylphs – Air spirits work with angels and help us connect to the spirit realm. They are said to protect our homes and look after our mental processes.

Undines – Found in natural water sources, these water spirits symbolize emotions and sensitivity and connect with us via dreams.

Salamanders – These fire spirits help us to raze the old to the ground and rise like a phoenix from the ashes.

Gnomes – Earth spirits put the colour in every flower, crystal and plant and help earth stay fertile and in balance.

HOW TO CONNECT WITH ELEMENTALS

- The most important step is belief – you must believe elementals exist in order to make a connection with them.

- The most obvious place to connect with them is in nature. Feel their presence around you and connect with them with your heart and soul or simply in your head. Elementals, like all other energy beings, can also communicate through feelings, as well as thoughts and healing.

- Care for the environment, nature and all living creatures.

- Try to practise love and gratitude in daily life, for example, by keeping a gratitude journal and writing down three things that you feel grateful for every night.

- Elementals are joyful and can feel a connection with you when you're playful, laughing and having fun.

- Ask if there's anything you can do to assist them in their work, ask them for signs, and ask for their help in whatever area you need it.

- Begin to build a rapport, and then stay in touch!

STARSEEDS

What is a starseed?

First described by Brad Steiger in his 1976 book *Gods of Aquarius*, Starseeds are believed to be advanced spiritual beings or extra-terrestrials that have come from other planets and realms. They are said to arrive on earth through reincarnation, taking human form at birth, and possess a wealth of spiritual and scientific knowledge dating back hundreds of thousands of years. Their mission here is to bring light and healing to humans and planet earth. They carry out their quest by helping humans raise their energy vibrations, demonstrating by example how humans can be more compassionate to themselves, others and the planet and awaken their own consciousness. More compassionate, spiritually enlightened humans benefit the planet's evolution.

Starseeds are not usually able to remember their true origin so that they can assimilate to life on earth, but they will, at some point, go through a process of awakening in order to fulfil their purpose.

AM I A STARSEED?

Does something about the word "starseed" resonate with you? If you have several of the common characteristics listed below, you may be one.

- You're always gazing at the stars.

- You're a deep thinker who constantly questions the "whys" of existence and the universe.

- You often feel like you don't belong and have always felt different.

- You're always searching for somewhere to call home, as you never feel at home wherever you are.

- You're an empath with strong intuition and psychic abilities.

- Animals and babies are drawn to you.

- People often describe you as an "an old soul".

- You know you're here for a reason, but it takes you a long time to find out what it is.

- You have a problem with systems and authority because you don't believe in being enslaved to anything.

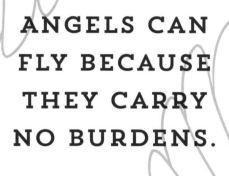

ANGELS CAN
FLY BECAUSE
THEY CARRY
NO BURDENS.

EILEEN ELIAS FREEMAN

TYPES OF STARSEED

Below are some of the main types of starseed:

- **Sirian** – Originating from the stars Sirius A and Sirius B, Sirians are said to have initiated the awakening of all human beings. Ascended masters like Jesus and Mother Mary are believed to have come from Sirius A.

- **Pleiadian** – Originates from the Pleiades, a star cluster also known as Seven Sisters and part of the Taurus constellation. Pleiadians are the record keepers for earth and hang out in a fifth-dimensional frequency, the birthplace of love and creativity. Matriarchal, they're here to help earth expand its consciousness.

- **Arcturian** – Arcturus is the brightest star in the Boötes constellation and its souls are the most advanced civilization in our galaxy. They are emotionally and mentally advanced and were intended to be the spiritual shamans and healers for humanity.

- **Andromedan** – Kind, loving and telepathic, from the spiral-shaped Andromeda galaxy, also known as MS31 or M31. These lovely beings are here to bring peace and love. Their balance of heart and intellect gives them a unique value in the universe.

- **Indigo, Crystal or Rainbow** – These individuals often possess special or supernatural abilities. Indigos embody the power of Archangel Michael, while Crystals carry the light and clarity of Archangel Gabriel. Rainbow children are the most recent wave of healing souls to come to earth and are often diagnosed with some form of autism.

- **Lightworker** – Lightworkers originate from a variety of planets and realms and incarnate to raise consciousness, helping earth and other worlds evolve. They spread kindness and love, always working towards the light.

- **Lemurian and Atlantean** – Lemuria and Atlantis were once highly advanced civilizations on earth, developing incredible spiritual and healing technologies. They have learned from past mistakes and are here to commit to positive innovation and advancement.

THE BEAUTY OF
ANGELS REMAINS
UNDIMMED,
EVEN IN YOUR
DARKEST HOUR

CHAPTER
THREE

CONNECTING WITH ANGELS

This chapter offers practical advice on ways to access
angelic help and guidance, looking at a range of different
methods to assist you in getting to know your angels
and spirit guides, from making a first connection to
developing a daily relationship. There are many ways
that angels and spirit guides can communicate with us:
via signs and signals and meditation and divination tools,
such as angel cards and crystals.
This chapter will help you to develop your intuition
and to confidently welcome angels and spirit guides
into your life. Let this be the beginning of
some beautiful relationships.

ASKING ANGELS FOR HELP

There will be plenty of occasions when you'll feel the need to call on angels, for example, if you're going through a stressful time or could do with some guidance over a confusing issue.

If you'd like guidance, focus on a question you'd like help with, either by asking it out loud or by writing it down. Go over this question several times and concentrate fully so that you give it your full attention. Make sure your question is as clear and succinct as possible to avoid any crossed wires.

Angels are most likely to respond in the form of signs. They might suddenly make themselves known or felt in some way, or they will leave subtle clues to guide you in the right direction. They may not do this immediately, so know that the signs will come in their own time, usually when you're ready to receive them.

ANGELS ARE
NEVER TOO
DISTANT TO
HEAR YOU

COMMON SIGNS OF AN ANGEL'S VISIT

- **Finding feathers** – seeing or finding a white feather is said to be a sign that an angel has heard your prayer or is offering protection, love and support at this time.

- **Animal visits** – you may notice a particular animal continually showing up in your life, either symbolically or physically. Perhaps there is a fox that visits your garden every evening, or you're drawn to watching a specific animal on a single occasion. Animals are said to carry messages from angels and are often reminders that an angel is watching over you.

- **Repeating numbers** – noticing the same number, or a repeating number sequence, such as 333, could be an angel sign. See pages 94–96 for a guide to the meaning of each number.

- **Meaningful messages** – did a book open at the right page with a message you needed to hear? Pay attention to any message that you hear repeatedly from different sources, as there may be a deeper meaning in it for you.

- **Dreams** – angels find it easier to communicate with you when your subconscious mind is open and relaxed, and sleep is the perfect state in which to receive messages. Pay particular attention to any recurring themes or images in your dreams.

- **Clouds** – have you ever looked at the sky and seen a cloud in the shape of an animal, a heart or one that looks like an angel? Whatever shape appears, consider whether this symbol has a special significance for you, as it could be an angelic message.

- **Scents** – have you ever noticed a scent that you associate with a deceased loved one in the most random of places? While relatives who have passed over can reveal their presence with a familiar scent, archangels are said to reveal themselves in the scent of flowers.

- **Rainbows** – angels can appear as a rainbow, reminding you that you're loved and that better things are on the way.

Angels rarely communicate directly by voice, unlike some other spirit guides, but through signs.

OTHER REASONS FOR ANGEL SIGNS

As we have discovered, you can ask your angels for signs that they are near. But what if you notice signs when you didn't explicitly ask for them? You may see signs from your angels or spirit guides if:

- You're aligning with your true purpose and following a right path.

- You're ready to begin a healing process. Angels may appear to reassure you with their support and encouragement.

- You're feeling isolated and low. Your angels are telling you that you're unconditionally loved and supported.

- You're experiencing a spiritual awakening. You may notice more angel signs as you start to deepen your connection with the spirit realm and universe. As your vibration raises, you will be able to connect with more higher-vibration beings.

ANGEL NUMBERS

Have you ever seen 11:11 on the digital clock in your car, only to glance up and notice that the car in front of you also has the number 11 on its number plate? Repetitive number sequences that keep catching your attention are known as angel numbers and are said to be messages from above.

Using numbers is an easy way for angels to communicate with you. Whenever you see a particular sequence recurring, ask your angels what they are trying to tell you, and listen to your thoughts, feelings and visions as your angels will be guiding you through these. The more frequently you begin to notice signs from angels, the more often they'll appear. Once you become more adept at understanding them, you'll suddenly be seeing signs and messages all over the place.

Seeing angel numbers is like a comfort hug from your spirit team, patting you on the back and saying that you're doing great and that they're there to support you.

ANGEL NUMBER MEANINGS

Whether you connect these signs to angels, spirit guides or ancestors, or even a higher plane of your own consciousness, angel numbers are a useful way to let you know that you're on the right path. They can also help you to decode life experiences or give you valuable insight into a current situation. These digits can be repeated or may appear within a pattern.

0 – zero symbolizes the start of a new phase of your life, so look out for new opportunities and be prepared to make some big decisions!

1 – the universe is telling you to go ahead – set your intention and manifest it positively with the love and support of your angels or guides.

2 – two represents balance and harmony, trust and alignment, and encourages you to be loving and co-operative in your relationships. Now is a good time to reach out to someone in the physical or spiritual realm who can help you to move forward.

3 – three is the number of creation and completion and carries the vibration of the ascended masters. It encourages you to feel confident in expressing yourself and reminds you to use the gifts that were divinely given to you to find more abundance on all levels.

4 – four symbolizes practicality and equilibrium. Get your plans in order and take positive action toward your goals. This will help you to establish the solid foundations to achieve your desires.

5 – major changes could be on the horizon with this number and your angels are asking you to accept these positively as they'll work out for the best.

6 – six has the vibration of unconditional love and empathy and is a gentle reminder to treat yourself and others with kindness. Remember to maintain a balance between the material and the spiritual in order to create stability.

7 – lucky number seven confirms that you're on the right path; favourable times are ahead! Seven could also relate to spiritual awakening or development.

8 – eight is the symbol of infinity, and some believe they're receiving support from departed loved ones when they see this number. Eight is a positive sign of achievements and success, encouraging you to follow your intuition and fulfil your highest potential.

9 – nine could symbolize the end of a chapter in your life, but whatever you'd like to do next, whether it's change career or move to a different country, be assured the universe will support courageous choices.

PYTHAGORAS AND ANGEL NUMBERS

The idea of numbers carrying their own meanings and energy has a long and distinguished history. The Greek philosopher Pythagoras (*ca.* 570–490 BCE), whose theories tormented most of us during Maths class at school, saw everything in the universe as mathematically precise, including numbers. Each number, he said, has its own vibration and meaning. He also believed the order in which a sequence of numbers occurred was not random but significant. Therefore, Pythagoras explained, our reality is a physical manifestation of the energetic vibration of numbers.

In the early 2000s, author Doreen Virtue labelled these as "angel numbers", and the term stuck. The phenomenon of divining a message from a sequence of numbers, or repeated numbers, has grown ever since, and now many websites offer interpretations of number sequences.

INTERPRETING ANGEL NUMBERS

Just like the interpretation of anything you receive from the higher realms, from dreams to cloud shapes, as well as the generalized number definitions above, it's also good to consider your own intuition and the personal meaning something may have to you.

One person may see 11:11 as a sign to manifest the desire they've been mulling over, while another may take it as validation that they're on a correct path.

When you see an angel number or you've begun to notice the same one several times, note it down along with any thoughts, emotions or impressions that spring to mind. As with any esoteric practice, it's worth bearing in mind that these guidance tools also have an element of subjectivity, and numerology is no exception.

Free will and agency always come into play, and while the angel-number guide above (pages 94–96) will give you a starting point, it's important to listen to your own ideas. Developing your own understanding of the numbers will provide a shortcut next time a particular number appears, and you'll already know what it means to you. The more comfortable and familiar you become with the numbers, the more you'll be able to use them as a reliable guidance system, one that's unique to your own inner truths, and that will help your burgeoning connection with the spirit world.

You may repeatedly see the same number sequences over a period of months (as long as it takes for you to get the message!), or you may observe a sequence on just one occasion that strikes you as significant. The important thing is to pay attention.

ASK FOR HELP
FROM YOUR
ANGELS, AND
TRUST THAT YOUR
TEAM OF GUIDES
AND ANGELS WILL
HELP YOU AS YOU
TAKE EACH AND
EVERY STEP ON
YOUR PATH.

MELANIE BECKLER

WE ARE NEVER
SO LOST THAT
AN ANGEL CAN'T
FIND US

IMPROVING AN ANGEL OR SPIRIT GUIDE'S POWER IN YOUR LIFE

Working with an angel or spirit guide can enrich your life. Like any new relationship, it takes some time to get to know each other and will require commitment and perseverance as you learn to recognize your guide's personality and the way they communicate.

Here are some tips for getting to know your angel or guide:

Build a rapport

Start with some simple connection techniques, such as walking in nature, sitting quietly or meditating. It's important that your mind is relaxed and still so that your energy field is open to receiving any messages. It's also important not to have any expectations of which guide or angel might show up, as they will know what's most appropriate for you. Have patience, particularly if nothing is showing up at first. You may have to prove that you're serious about connection and that you're open to trusting and accepting whatever comes through.

Demonstrate your commitment to personal growth
As you begin to work with your guides more frequently, their communications will increase, and your ability to receive messages will improve. Common forms of communication from spirit guides are dreams and telepathy, as well as via meditation or using your intuition.

Keep a journal
Dedicate a specific journal to your communication with your angels or guides. Noting down any messages, feelings, emotions, smells, sensations, colours or anything else you intuit could be useful and help you to establish that you can trust both your intuition and your guides. It's important to write everything down as soon as possible and not worry about analyzing it. What you've received may not make sense now but may do somewhere down the line.

HOW TO ASK YOUR ANGEL OR SPIRIT GUIDE QUESTIONS

Once you've established a relationship with a regular guide or angel, you can begin asking specific questions. Your guide may be able to answer the question, or they may bring in another guide who is able to help. You can always ask your regular guide if there's a more appropriate angel or guide for a specific area of questioning.

You will come into contact with your wider circle of guides this way, and the more open you are to connecting with multiple guides, the more varied, entertaining and beneficial your experiences will be. Know that you are surrounded by many guides who have expertise in the areas you need and who want to help you. All you have to do is ask for their help and trust that they will come. You can also ask a guide a specific question just before going to sleep; they may answer in your dreams, so have your journal handy at your bedside, just in case.

WHEN ANGELS VISIT US, WE DO NOT HEAR THE RUSTLE OF WINGS, NOR FEEL THE FEATHERY TOUCH OF THE BREAST OF A DOVE; BUT WE KNOW THEIR PRESENCE BY THE LOVE THEY CREATE IN OUR HEARTS.

MARY BAKER EDDY

HOW TO PERFORM AN
ANGEL-CARD READING

The first documented use of tarot cards can be traced back to Italy around 1430, while oracle and angel cards are more modern adaptations. Angel cards are much easier and more straightforward for beginners than a traditional tarot deck. Angel-card readings offer guidance from the angelic realm and your pack will feature pictures of angels with an associated word or words.

Here are some quick and easy steps to perform your first reading:

1. "Season" the pack. Cleanse your deck of any previous energy and tune the cards to your energy instead. It's important to form a rapport with your personal set of cards. Cleanse the deck by smudging it (see page opposite) with sage or incense.

2. Flick through the deck, touching every card to transfer your energy onto it. This is also a way of establishing familiarity with the cards. You could also sleep with them beside your bed in order for your energies to synchronize.

3. Thank the angels for their guidance and know that every card you pick is meant for you or the person you're reading for.

4. All angel-card decks include an accompanying book to help you interpret the card you've chosen and offer guidance on what type of spreads you can use, ranging from picking one card daily, to a three- or nine-card spread for more in-depth readings.

At first, reading them can be daunting but practice makes perfect! Be sure to take note of your intuition too.

The ancient spiritual practice of smudging comes from the Native Americans, who used it as a purification ritual. Light a wad of dried white sage or palo santo (a sweet-smelling wood) and pass cards or crystals through the smoke to cleanse them or waft the smoke around a particular space or yourself to clear negative energies. Smudging tools can be found in many spiritual shops or online.

CONNECTING WITH ANGELS USING CRYSTALS

Some crystals have their own spirit guides or beings, but meditating with crystals can also facilitate wider contact with the angelic realm. Ideal crystals for this purpose include angelite, apophyllite, celestite, danburite, larimar, muscovite, petalite, phenacite, selenite, seraphinite and tanzanite. These stones may facilitate your connection with the angelic realm, but working with any crystal will help you to connect to higher energies.

Connecting with Archangel Raphael – prehnite is said to facilitate contact with Archangel Raphael and other higher-dimension or even extra-terrestrial beings.

Connecting with angels of truth and wisdom – the stunning light-blue colour of blue topaz is said to attune to the angels of truth and wisdom, helping you to see where you've drifted away from your own truths.

Connecting with ascended masters – moldavite, phenacite and tanzanite are particularly recommended for connection with the ascended masters.

EASY STEPS FOR ANGEL-CRYSTAL CONNECTION

Find a quiet place where you can relax. Lie down or sit comfortably and light some candles or incense if this is something you like to do.

1. Take in the colour and detail of your crystal. Hold it in your left hand or place it on the third eye, whichever feels the most natural to you. Close your eyes and visualize the colour and energy of the crystal filling your energy field.

2. Next, visualize a white or golden light of protection around you to protect you during your meditation.

3. Ask (either out loud or in your head) to connect to the angelic realm and for the angel that is most appropriate for you at this time to step forward.

4. Listen to any message the angel gives you or notice any images that you see. Feel free to ask your angel any question you need guidance with.

5. Note down anything you receive in a journal.

ARCHANGELS AND LIGHT RAYS

Each archangel is said to work within a specific light-ray (colour). The light waves for the seven angel colours are said to vibrate at different electromagnetic energy frequencies, attracting the angels whose energies correspond with that frequency. Each ray represents something, and, depending on the help you're seeking, you can choose to "tune in" to the appropriate light ray.

The rays and their associated archangels are:

- **Red:** Uriel – wise service
- **Pink:** Chamuel – love, peace
- **Purple:** Zadkiel – transformation, mercy
- **Yellow:** Jophiel – wisdom for making decisions
- **White:** Gabriel – purity, harmony, holiness
- **Blue:** Michael – protection, faith, courage, strength, power
- **Green:** Raphael – healing, prosperity

WORKING WITH ARCHANGELS MICHAEL AND RAPHAEL FOR HEALING

Working with Archangels Michael and Raphael can help heal pain stemming from fear, of which physical illness can be a manifestation. Raphael's speciality is healing, one of Michael's is courage. Meditating with them both can empower you with the courage to overcome your fear and guide you in your healing.

1. Ask Michael to show you which fear may be creating physical pain. If it stems from having to deal with the pain, ask for peace as you try to heal.

2. Give yourself permission to let go of the fear so that your body becomes receptive to healing.

3. In her book *Quantum Angel Healing*, Eva-Maria Mora suggests asking Michael the following: "Please come with your sword of light and cut all negative energetic connections with persons, situations, places, and objects that are harmful for me and/or rob me of my life force energy."

4. Ask Raphael to send his healing energy to relieve the pain.

RELIEVING PAIN WITH ARCHANGEL RAPHAEL

Raphael and his angels can help to dissolve negative energy and replace it with positive energies that encourage healing. When you ask Raphael for assistance, he and his angels will work within the green light ray (associated with the heart chakra) and infuse the body and its aura with love and high-vibration healing energy.

1. Prepare yourself for meditation or prayer as you usually would. Begin by asking three times if what you're connecting to is the energy of Archangel Raphael. Every time you ask the question, you should receive a "yes" in reply. If you receive a "no" or a cryptic answer that isn't a direct yes, ask that entity to kindly leave and return to the light and continue trying until you connect with Raphael.

2. Talk to Raphael about the pain you're experiencing. Feel free to chat to him as if he's a friend and ask for his help and guidance.

3. Ask him to help you identify anything specific

that may have caused your pain. Sometimes pain has a physical cause (such as a fall or a car accident) but in other cases, mental or emotional factors such as stress and fear could have created a problem.

4. If you discover that fear is a potential root cause of your malady, you can ask Archangel Michael to help you in overcoming this fear (see page 111).

5. You can then invite Raphael to send healing energy to the painful area. You may see emerald green light in your mind's eye as he and his angels work, or you can visualize this colour surrounding the area that's troubling you or ripple it through your whole energy field.

6. Bathe in the positive energy for as long as you are intuitively guided to. Give thanks to Archangel Raphael and his angels and know that you can ask him for help as often as you need.

OTHER WAYS RAPHAEL MAY ASSIST

Breathwork

Raphael is connected with the air element, so he may direct you to focus on your breathing. Deep and conscious breaths can lower stress and foster healing. In his book on communicating with Raphael for healing, Richard Webster advises blowing gently on any afflicted area, visualizing it becoming whole and perfect again, while feeling Raphael's energy flowing through you.

Exercise and diet

Exercise is an important element in strengthening the body to assist its health and vitality. Raphael can suggest specific and appropriate methods of physical exercise. He may also suggest dietary changes to relieve pain and the pressure on your body.

It's important to have no expectations about how healing will occur. Your prayer will be heard and answered, but be open to the way or time sequence in which healing may be given.

WORKING WITH ARCHANGEL URIEL AND THE RED RAY

Uriel and the red ray represent wise service and truth. Uriel's name means "light of God" and he'll illuminate your path but may also reveal cracks in your life. Ask Uriel for help with decision making and letting go of damaging emotions, and for the wisdom to identify dangerous situations, recognize your self-worth and liberate yourself from abusive situations.

Prayer suggestions

- Ask for the compassion, courage and strength to complete tasks in service of God or others, and ask for guidance in specific tasks

- Unearth the talents you've been gifted in order to make your contribution

- Ask for help with seeing the truth of a situation

Symbols of communication from Uriel

- Number sequences 1, 11, 111, 1111

- Sparks, inexplicable light flickers, thunderstorms

- A desire to help others or improve yourself, seeing a course of action clearly

Crystals for connection: amber, fire opal, tiger's eye

WORKING WITH ARCHANGEL CHAMUEL AND THE PINK RAY

The pink ray symbolizes love and peace, while Chamuel represents unconditional love and peaceful relationships. Ask Chamuel for help with inner peace and resolving conflicts, forgiveness, finding or nurturing romantic love and letting go of negative emotions.

Prayer suggestions

- Ask for help with maintaining loving relationships of all types
- Ask for help with forgiveness
- Ask to improve your compassion
- Ask for help if looking for a romantic partner

Symbols of communication from Chamuel

- Seeing the colour pink everywhere
- Noticing traditional symbols of love, such as hearts

Crystals for connection: rose quartz, emerald, fluorite

WORKING WITH ARCHANGEL ZADKIEL AND THE PURPLE RAY

Zadkiel and the purple ray represent mercy, transformation and positive change. Ask Zadkiel for help with confessing sins and approaching God for mercy, forgiving others, healing emotional wounds, and making positive changes.

Prayer suggestions
- Ask for assistance in developing your spiritual path
- Ask for help to forgive both yourself and others
- Work with the violet flame to cleanse negative energies

Symbols of communication from Zadkiel
- Noticing the colour purple
- Working with the violet flame
- Letting go of resentment towards someone or feel lighter
- Seeing things in a different light
- Experiencing a deeper connection to the spiritual realm

Crystals for connection: amethyst, blue lace agate, lapis lazuli, blue chalcedony

WORKING WITH ARCHANGEL JOPHIEL AND THE YELLOW RAY

Jophiel and the yellow ray represent wisdom and illumination. Her name means "Beauty of God" and she can help you see beauty in every situation. Ask Jophiel for help with experiencing joy, wisdom to make decisions, overcoming unhealthy thought patterns, illuminating the truth of a situation and recognizing your inner beauty.

Prayer suggestions

- Ask for help with letting go of negative attitudes and emotions

- Ask for insight into seeing situations from a higher perspective

- Ask for help to absorb the information you need to learn

- Ask for inspiration for new creative projects

Symbols of communication from Jophiel

- Being mesmerized by the beauty around you

- Noticing lots of yellow in your environment

Crystals for connection: citrine, ametrine, rutilated quartz

WORKING WITH ARCHANGEL GABRIEL AND THE WHITE RAY

Archangel Gabriel and the white ray represent purity and harmony that come from holiness, as well as revelation. Ask Gabriel for help with understanding God's messages, clarity, wise decision making, communicating effectively, raising children and improving confidence.

Prayer suggestions
- Ask for help to cleanse your life of negative attitudes, behaviours and addictions

- Ask for guidance with your personal and spiritual growth

- Ask for assistance to let go of your insecurities

- Ask for help with developing your communication skills

- Ask for inspiration for artistic projects

Symbols of communication from Gabriel
- Direct visitations Virgin Mary style (but these are quite unlikely)!

- Feeling compelled to make a fresh start

- Feeling a desire to pursue the truth of a situation

Crystals for connection: angelite, celestite, larimar, blue chalcedony

WORKING WITH ARCHANGEL MICHAEL AND THE BLUE RAY

Archangel Michael and the blue ray represent protection, faith, courage, strength and power. Michael is said to be the leader of all holy angels. Ask Michael for help with protection, defending yourself, courage to overcome fears and strength to overcome temptation.

Prayer suggestions
- Ask for help with finding your purpose in life and the courage to achieve it
- Ask for assistance in dealing with challenges
- Ask Michael for help in developing leadership qualities

Symbols of communication from Michael
- You may "hear his voice" during a crisis or get a gut feeling
- Seeing lots of blue
- You may feel warmth or a tingling sensation
- A feeling or sensation of peace may wash over you

Crystals for connection: blue topaz, aquamarine, turquoise, light blue sapphire

WORKING WITH ARCHANGEL RAPHAEL AND THE GREEN RAY

Raphael and the green ray represent healing and prosperity. Ask Raphael for help with healing of any kind and increased prosperity in any area of life.

Prayer suggestions

- Ask Raphael to send healing, from physical injuries to mental, spiritual or emotional scars

- Ask Raphael to help you with the strength to be an active participant in your own healing

- Seek help and support with any money concerns you have

Symbols of communication from Raphael

- Feeling a powerful healing energy around you or entering your body

- Seeing the colour green, potentially around the area that needs healing

- Humorous signs via everyday objects, such as a relevant message on a license plate or book

- Ringing in your ear

- An urge to spend time in nature

Crystals for connection: malachite, aventurine, selenite

CONNECTING WITH ARCHANGELS USING CANDLES

Some people find that lighting a candle of the same ray colour that they're praying with helps them to focus on the colour itself and brings a sense of stillness. Not only can candles be comforting and peaceful but their light symbolizes guidance, hope, faith and the desire for illumination. The different colour frequencies of the candles match the vibrations of the relevant angel working in that light ray.

Open mind

It's important to keep an open mind when asking angels for guidance as they can deliver what you need in many ways. While you may feel healing directly during a prayer to Raphael, for example, most often Raphael's angels will work through guiding the medical professionals around you. You may receive signs within the next week or so after prayer, ranging from inspiring new ideas that seem to come from nowhere to something you read in a magazine that feels appropriate to your situation.

MUSIC IS WELL
SAID TO BE
THE SPEECH
OF ANGELS.

THOMAS CARLYLE

CONCLUSION

Working with your angel or spirit guides can be life-changing, from offering you comfort in your darkest hour to guiding you towards your purpose in life.

There are so many different guides we can call upon not just in our hour of need but every day, and each angel or guide that we work with is able to offer us specific expertise tailored to our needs and circumstances, no matter how big or small. It's a wonderful blessing to have friends like these.

We've looked at many different types of angels, archangels and other spirit guides in this book – how they can help you and how to connect with them.

We've also explored how different belief systems view angelic or celestial beings and the fundamental importance they have in many religious traditions.

Hopefully this book has given you the confidence to begin or deepen your relationship with your angelic or celestial friends. Remember that they are always listening and always by your side, ready to help – all you have to do is ask. As you discover many new beautiful relationships and start to see the results of how they can enrich your life, you'll never look back. Wishing you love and light on your journey!

THE LITTLE BOOK OF GODDESSES
Astrid Carvel

ISBN: 978-1-80007-198-8

Embrace the power of the divine in this beginner's guide to some of mythology's fiercest females and most legendary ladies. Learn about Athena, the Greek goddess of wisdom and war; Bastet, the Egyptian goddess of pleasure and protection; Freyja, the Norse goddess of love, and many others. You'll be inspired and empowered by the tales of feminine power, strength and wisdom of all these dazzling deities.

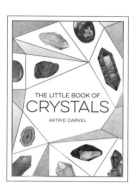

THE LITTLE BOOK OF CRYSTALS
Astrid Carvel

ISBN: 978-1-78685-959-4

Crystals have long been used for holistic healing purposes. Every crystal emits vibrations, which can help to bring balance, calm and positivity into your life. This guide will teach you how to select and maintain your crystals, along with basic techniques for crystal meditation and balancing your chakras, to bring harmony to mind, body and spirit. Discover over 40 crystals, their unique properties and how to make use of their power in everyday life.

Have you enjoyed this book? If so, find us on
Facebook at **Summersdale Publishers**,
on Twitter at **@Summersdale** and on Instagram
at **@summersdalebooks** and get in touch.
We'd love to hear from you!

www.summersdale.com

IMAGE CREDITS